Jason,

It's a pleasure to talk with you

Brian

GETTING
PAST ME
AND
BEING CLOSER
TO THEE

A CLEAR PATH TO A MORE SPIRITUAL AND HAPPIER LIFE

BRIAN THOMAS

ISBN 978-1-64191-197-9 (paperback)
ISBN 978-1-64191-240-2 (hardcover)
ISBN 978-1-64191-198-6 (digital)

Christian Faith Publishing, Inc.
832 Park Avenue
Meadville, PA 16335
www.christianfaithpublishing.com

Printed in the United States of America

Contents

Introduction

Many people are looking for something in their life that they have yet to find. There is a vague emptiness that defies to be filled. Money, fame, power, security, or earthly pleasures still leave a void. Maybe it could be summed up this way: "All my life my heart has sought a thing I cannot name." This was found on the wall of a one-room apartment in a rundown apartment building housing hippies, winos, and street people in the sixties. It was on colored art paper, and the words were covered in glitter. Someone in this down-and-out place probably at a time in their life when they were as down and out as the place they lived in created this and hung it on the wall. It was the only thing in an otherwise bare room. Whoever came up with this was probably at one of the lowest points in their life and was digging deep into their soul and being.

They are not alone. How many people are there who are looking for something they cannot find because they don't even know what they are looking for? "All my life my heart has sought a thing I cannot name."

Maybe the answer lies inside of us. It must be something we can't see or touch, but it's there. It isn't part of our physical being, but it is still within us. It is beyond ourselves. It isn't in or even a part of our physical world. Something tells us it's there, and so we seek it at a time when we feel we have nothing else. "All of my life my heart has sought a thing I cannot name." No one can tell us what it is. No one can put a name on it. If this thing we cannot name is anywhere, it is in our spirit. This is only where true peace and joy can be found. Is this not the true deep-seated desire of every living human being to live in peace with joy?

Our nature dictates that we are primarily concerned with ourselves before anybody or anything. This doesn't mean that we can't care about others or put things aside. We can and we do, but our self-preservation is still our top priority, the *Me*. It's still all about "*Me*" and what we want and need. It is our basic nature, and that doesn't change. What we can change is to put aside the "*Me*" to some degree. We do this when we love another person. We do this when we put aside a dependence on drug or alcohol. The quest to become a spiritual person means putting the *Me* aside so you can be closer to God. It also means putting worldly things aside, at least some of them. We can have less and still be happy. We don't have to have the biggest house, the most expensive car, the finest furniture, or a clothes closet that takes up a small room. The secret lies in moderation of all things. We cannot do without worldly things, but we can do with less. We don't have to live in or practice poverty to be spiritual. We don't have to put ourselves completely aside to be a spiritual person, and we don't have to practice chastity to attain spirituality. This book is about finding a way to be a more spiritual that is within our power to do as human beings.

Purpose

The purpose of this book is to bring one person closer to God so they will have true joy and peace in their life. We can only try to be a better person than we were and are. There is hope for everyone no matter who you are or what you have done.

A Sinner's Plea

All of my life has been about me
So it was very difficult for me to see
What was right in front of my eyes
Making up and believing my own lies
Such as I never had enough
I always needed and wanted more stuff
I treated people like they were Dixie cups
I used them and tossed them away like unwanted pups
My ego knew no bounds, all was fair
As long as I got more than my share, I did not despair
This is the life I had chosen to lead
Not knowing that I had planted a seed
One that would cut me down to size
And lead ultimately to my own demise
Now I'm trying to get past me
And get as close as I can to thee.

There Are No Atheists in Foxholes

It's an old saying, "There are no atheist in foxholes." When bullets are whizzing inches from your head and bombs are exploding on every side of you within a few feet, something changes in you. You are alone, and your life is in eminent danger. When there is nothing between you and death, your whole being cries out for help. There is nothing or no one to help you in this time or peril, and as a last resort, you turn to God.

There is nothing else left to believe in. Out of pure necessity, you turn to and are forced by your circumstances to believe in God. You must believe God is your only salvation at this time. There is nothing else to believe in. "There are no atheists in foxholes."

Should an EMP (electromagnetic pulse) bomb explode a mile high over Kansas City, every electrical and electronic device in this country from coast to coast will be fried and useless. Since everything is tied to computers—our gasoline, utilities, lights, water, phone, food distribution, manufacturing, farming and retail outlets—we will be without food, in the dark, without water, communication or a way to travel and go places because the gasoline pumps will not function.

We will in effect be in the Stone Age. All of our possessions will have little or no meaning. Ninety percent of us will be dead in a year, either from starvation or from being killed for what little food we have. This will be the time when the great majority of people turn to God for help.

Some will be saved from death; most won't. It will be, however, a time to have the opportunity to believe in and get closer to God before death.

Being close to God means choosing between the world of materialism, pleasures, ego, and God. Since the material world will be for the most part destroyed, choosing God over the world will be made much easier. We will have nothing to cling to except our faith, love, and trust in God. God will become our reality. We will have a last chance to set things right with God before death takes us. The world we presently live in is so filled with materialism, pleasures, and ego fulfillment that the choice becomes almost too great to deal with. Most only become spiritual and see God as we are taking our last breath. There is a way to become more spiritual even though we are inundated by the lure of this materialistic, pleasurable, self-obsessed world. There is a balance that can be struck. We must take into account that we as humans are very susceptible to worldly things because of all the physical and psychological needs which are tied to our need to survive. Our number one and greatest instinct is survival. We have other instincts but none as great as the need to survive. Every cell in our body needs food, oxygen, and stimulation. These needs and how we meet them control what we do and how we choose to do it. To survive, we must feed these millions of cells, provide them with food, oxygen, and stimulation. In our body besides all of these cells is a spirit. Our cells will die. Our spirit never dies. Our spirit is connected to us as a part of God. Most of us are not even aware that we have spiritual needs also. Our spirit needs peace, balance, and harmony with our physical and mental being. Balance is the key word here because we are caught between two worlds, the physical and spiritual. We need to fulfill our physical needs, but we also need to fulfill our spiritual needs. The physical will someday die, the spiritual will live forever.

There are ways to achieve this balance, and if you are of a mind to find balance with the reward of peace within, then these guidelines will be laid out for you. It is up to you to choose how much spiritual and how much physical you want in your life and how close you want to be with God.

The Book

A great speaker came to the church I was attending one Sunday. He had a sense of humor, was fluent, and you could tell by his remarks that he was very well read. During the course of his speaking, he mentioned that he had over five thousand books in his library. He went on to say that if he had only one book he could keep out of the five thousand, there would be no doubt in his mind which one he would keep. This is a very strong endorsement for a man so well read of all kinds of literature and especially Christian writings. Most people may not even have heard of this book much less read it, especially Protestants. The reason for that is because it was written by a Catholic monk in the fourteenth century. It is part of the religious writings by Catholic authors. Remember this book is the only book a Protestant preacher would keep out of all the religious books he has read. This is a very, very strong recommendation for a Protestant preacher to endorse a book written by a Catholic.

Obviously, this is no ordinary book but one that has been a huge amount of spiritual inspiration since it was first written hundreds of years ago. This book, which most people are not even aware of, has been translated into more languages than any other book except the Bible. It is one of Christianity's best kept secret.

It was written by Thomas A. Kempis who was born in the lower Rhine town of Kempis, Germany, which is where part of his name came from, in 1380. His father was a blacksmith, and his mother a schoolmistress. His given name means little hammer in German. When he was nineteen, he entered the monastery of St. Agnes in Holland where he spent the rest of his life until he died in 1471. He took the vows of poverty, chastity, and obedience when he entered the monastery and lived his life in almost total obscurity. He read, wrote, prayed, and heard the confessions of people who came to the monastery. His book is all about how to love God. It is free from all intellectual pretensions and probes beneath the surface of our being. The book is divided into four books.

The first book has to do with the withdrawal of our earthly life. It emphasizes the spiritual life and renounces all that is vain about our life, our ego, our materialism, and our passions as being nothing more than illusions.

Book two, *Directions for a Spiritual Life*, teaches us how to have inward peace, purity of heart, and a good conscience. It also shows us how by moderating our longing and desires along with practicing patience we can become closer to God. Book three emphasizes a total acceptance of and giving of yourself to God. This is the part that deals with getting past yourself and leaving yourself behind.

Book four, *On the Blessed Sacrament*, shows us that when God resides in and is allowed to control our heart, we can put aside our own pleasures and desires.

We would be united with God and have peace. When we offer ourselves purely and completely to God, all of our sins will be washed away.

This book can help you attain what every human being wants and that is peace within ourselves. This book will help you achieve peace of mind. Read a chapter of this book every day which is usually only one page, as a daily devotional and spiritual guide. The name of the book is The Imitation of Christ by Thomas 'A Kempis.

Famous Sayings
by Thomas 'A. Kempis

The acknowledgment of our weakness is the first step in repairing our lost line.

Out of sight, out of mind. The absent are always in the wrong.

Be not angry that you cannot make others as you wish them to be, since you cannot make yourself as you wish to be.

Great tranquility of heart is his who cares for neither praise nor blame.

First keep peace with yourself, then you can also bring peace to others.

Love feels no burden, thinks nothing of trouble, attempts what is above its strength, pleads no excuse of impossibility, for it thinks all things lawful for itself and all things possible.

What most of all hinders heavenly consolation is that you are too slow in turning yourself to prayer.

If you cannot mold yourself entirely as you wish, how can you expect other people to be entirely to your liking?

Oh, how great peace and quietness would he possess who should cut off all vain anxiety and place all his confidence in God.

A humble knowledge of thyself is a surer way to God than a deep search after learning. We usually know what we can do, but temptation shows us who we are.

The loftier the building, the deeper must the foundation be laid.

Gladly we desire to make other men perfect, but we will not amend our own fault.

He will easily be content and at peace whose conscience is pure.

All men commend patience although few are willing to practice it.

A man is hindered and distracted in proportion as he draws outward things to himself.

Man proposes, but God disposes.

I would far rather feel remorse than know how to define it.

Never be entirely idle, but either be reading or writing or praying or meditating or endeavoring something for the public good.

Blaise Pascal and the Wager

Blaise Pascal, who was born in 1623, is considered to have one of the most brilliant minds of all time. He was a mathematician, inventor, physician, religious philosopher, and a renowned writer of prose.

Besides writing one of the greatest classics of philosophy entitled *Les Provinciales*, Pascal had the passionate conviction of a man in love with the absolute who saw no solution apart from a heartfelt desire for the truth together with a love of God that works continuously toward destroying all self-love. Pascal believed morality cannot be separated from spirituality.

Pascal's Inventions and Conceptions

- laid the foundation for the modern theory of probabilities
- conceived and constructed a calculating device which was the first digital calculator
- invented the syringe
- created the hydraulic press
- laid the foundation for the calculus of probabilities
- conceived the first wrist watch
- invented the roulette machine when working on a concept to create a perpetual motion device
- was the inventor of the Pascaline which was the earliest form of the modern computer
- wrote the *Pensées*—the purpose of the book was to overcome the skeptic by means of a wager.

Pascal believed that men must be brought to God through Jesus Christ alone because a creature could never know the infinite if Jesus had not descended to assume the proportion of man's fallen state.

Life is a gamble. Every time you make a choice you are gambling. Will it be the right one? What are the odds? Sometimes the odds are in your favor and then again at times they aren't. There is no such thing as a sure thing. Blaise Pascal was a brilliant scientist and mathematician, a genius born in France on June 19, 1623. He invented the calculator, the forerunner of today's computer. He discovered and proved that the vacuum does exist, and he formulated laws of chance and probability which are still in use in today's world.

On November 28, 1654, he had a two-hour ecstatic vision that led to his conversion. He became a true believer in the divinity of Jesus Christ, and as a result came up with what is now known as Pascal's Wager. The concept is simple yet irrefutable. It is framed in the context of a bet, a bet which everyone must make during their life. It is the most important bet anyone will ever make because so much is riding on it. Place your bet.

Pascal's Wager

The most important bet you will ever make is going to be forced upon you. There is no way to get out of it. You must bet one way or the other. This is the bet.

1. If you believe in God and you are wrong, you lose nothing.

    Let's say you bet that there is a God and Jesus Christ was divine. What happens if you're wrong? There is no God, Jesus Christ was not divine, and a life after death does not exist. You lose, but what have you lost? Nothing. You will have lost nothing.

2. If you don't believe in God and you are right, you gain nothing.

    Suppose that you bet that there is no God and that Jesus Christ was just another man. Let's say you are absolutely right and win the bet. What do you win? Nothing. You will gain nothing for your wager.

3.   If you don't believe in God and you are wrong, you have lost everything.

If, on the other hand, you choose not to believe and reject God and you're wrong you will have chosen to spend eternity without God, your eternity could be spent alone and in the dark with the torment of an awareness of what you have lost, that in an eternity that has no end.

4.   If you believe in God and you are right, you gain everything.

On the other hand, suppose you bet that God and Christ do exist and that there is life after death and you are right and win the bet, what did you win? Everything. The winner of this bet will spend eternity with God, whose love is unconditional, all-encompassing, and infinite. There is no end to God's love. You will spend eternity being loved and feeling a love that will far surpass any joy and ecstasy that you have ever felt. Your eternity, of which there is no end, will be spent in absolute peace, freedom, and harmony with the never-ending bliss of being loved by the greater love of all.

You have no choice but to bet. You are either betting that there is a god and a life after death or you are wagering that there is a no God and when you die it's the end of you, there is nothing else. In this matter you have no choice but to make a choice. You will have to place your bet one way or the other.

You are reading this so you are still alive and have time to place your bet. It doesn't matter what you have done with your life before now. God loves you, always has, always will, and this love is unconditional and includes absolute forgiveness. Everyone on Earth strives for the same thing to feel good. When you open your heart to God and let him come into your heart and life, you will feel better than you have ever felt. Your life will change and become better and better. Place your bet on God and his love for you. You have everything to gain and nothing to lose.

Famous Quotes
from Blaise Pascal

Love has reasons which reason cannot understand.

Small minds are concerned with the extraordinary, great minds with the ordinary.

Noble deeds that are concealed are most esteemed.

The sensitivity of men to small matters, and their indifference to great ones, indicates a strange inversion.

Men despise religion. They hate it and are afraid it may be true.

The greatness of man is great in that he knows himself to be wretched. A tree does not know itself to be wretched.

Time heals griefs and quarrels, for we change and are no longer the same persons. Neither the offender nor the offended are any more themselves.

Do you wish people to think well of you? Don't speak well of yourself.

There are only two kinds of men: the righteous who think they are sinners and the sinners who think they are righteous.

Since we cannot know all that there is to be known about anything, we ought to know a little about everything.

We sail within a vast sphere, ever drifting in uncertainty, driven from end to end.

We are only falsehood, duplicity, contradiction; we both conceal and disguise ourselves from ourselves.

All men's miseries derive from not being able to sit in a quiet room alone.

Men never do evil so completely and cheerfully as when they do it from religious conviction.

Belief is a wise wager. Granted that faith cannot be proved, what harm will come to you if you gamble on its truth, and it proves false? If you gain, you gain all; if you lose, you lose nothing. Wager, then, without hesitation, that He exists.

Man's greatness lies in his power of thought.

The least movement is of importance to all nature. The entire ocean is affected by a pebble.

Thus so wretched is man that he would weary, even without any cause for weariness... and so frivolous is he that, though full of a thousand reasons for weariness, the least thing, such as playing billiards or hitting a ball, is sufficient enough to amuse him.

Happiness is neither without us nor within us. It is in God, both without us and within us.

Truth is so obscure in these times, and falsehood so established, that, unless we love the truth, we cannot know it.

Who We Are and What We Are

1. Before we ask who we are we must first find out what we are, we are first and foremost human beings with a human body. It is a scientific fact that we are composed of over 90 percent water. Water is a combination of hydrogen and oxygen atoms. The average person is comprised of nearly two thousand trillion oxygen cells inside of us. This is more numerous than the leaves in every forest on Earth.

    The sphere encompassed by the electron in the atoms contains millions of yards of nothingness since over 90 percent of every atom is empty space.

    Rather than the solid mass we seem to be, we are nothing more than a porous froth of atomic Styrofoam. The tiny central nucleus of the atom is so dense that if your body could be packed with deflated atoms rather than the empty ones that comprise your body now, the tip of one of your fingers would weigh close to a billion tons. This is a scientific fact. What does all of this mean? It means that we are simply big sacs of water, and over 95 percent of us is empty space. Our human bodies are basically an illusion of solidity, and if you still feel you are special then consider the fact that there are millions of water sacs just like yourself that inhabit the Earth we live on. And if you still feel special after knowing all the above then consider this one last scientific fact. If all of your oxygen atoms were to vanish you would still be visible but not for very long. The mist of leftover elements would scatter with the first puff of wind. This is what we are as human beings. We have limited life spans and then this human body eventually evaporates into nothingness leaving only our spiritual being. We are but dust in the wind.

Who We Are

2. We are what we think and what we do, nothing more. It doesn't matter who people think we are, it only matters who we really are. Once you understand what we are, it's easy to understand why we live only a limited time in this world.

    We are two beings in one, we are a human being and a spiritual being. On our human side, the only reason we are able to move, see, hear, speak, and understand is because we have life inside of us. This life is in the form of a soul or spirit. This soul belongs to us, but the essence of this soul is God. This is our spiritual being. God is in our soul, and part of it so when God leaves our soul, the life leaves our body, and we die. Our human being comes to an abrupt end. Our soul which belongs to us and to us alone at this point continues to live and has eternal life. God gave us this soul and gave us life in both human and spiritual. He was for us and always will be a part of our soul.

    Our desire to become closer to our spirit or soul is also a desire to become closer to God and experience the everlasting life and the infinite love, peace, and joy which only God can provide.

The Seven Deadly Sins

The Seven Heavenly Virtues and Everything in Between

The seven deadly sins are wrath, pride, greed, sloth, envy, gluttony, and lust.

The *seven heavenly virtues* are love, humility, generosity, work, gladness, fasting, and chastity.

The seven deadly sins are the extremes of the world we live in. They represent the worst within us that is taken to its very limit. Each deadly sin has a degree of evil and separation from God. They cannot kill our souls, but they can deaden them. They can cause our souls to be black with no light. This is the farthest we can be removed from God. The sin is what we have done to ourselves and others in the quest to gain the ultimate. The seven deadly sins are the ultimate of human depravity to which we can sink. When we indulge our self to the limit in any one of the seven deadly sins we have removed ourselves as far as we can form God. There are, however, degrees of each one that no matter how dedicated we are to being a spiritual person that we indulge in.

The seven deadly sins should be called the seven deadly temptations. Each one is a temptation to our human nature which has certain needs, wants, and desires. As Thomas A. Kemps so well put it, "We usually know what we can do, but temptation shows us who we are."

Each deadly sin has a heavenly virtue that is the exact opposite of the deadly sin. Each of the deadly sins have degrees that starts off with the worst and ends with a heavenly virtue.

Less than 5 percent of all people fall into the absolute state of sin or evil and less than 5 percent of all people fall into the state of absolute virtue. Over 90 percent of all people fall into varying degrees of moderation between the two. This is because absolute evil is impossible, and absolute virtue is equally just as impossible. Our spiritual quest must be based on the reality of our human nature which at best is imperfect and therefore a true spirituality is possible only when acting in moderation.

Sometimes we are so wrapped up in materialism that it is a part of us and a way of life. We are surrounded by it. That's why it is a difficult choice to put worldly goods aside for the sake of spirituality. Again, everything is in degrees and moderation. We can become less materialistic and more spiritual by putting aside the things that we may not truly need. We can't put everything aside or most things aside, but we can put some things aside. We can become more spiritual when we do that. In the process we must put ourselves aside to get past "*me*".

The following statements are true when it comes to finding a clear path to spirituality:

1. Material possessions do not bring you closer to God.
2. Physical pleasure does not bring you closer to God.
3. Acclaim and recognition by other people do not bring you closer to God.
4. When we die, our never-ending destiny is now in the hands of God depending on how close we are to him.
5. The trick is to do something in moderation that makes you feel good and brings you closer to God.

The Deadly Sin of Envy and the Heavenly Virtue of Joy

The Deadly Sin of Envy

Definition: A feeling of discontent and resentment aroused by the contemplation of another's desirable possessions or qualities with a strong desire to have them for one's self, the possession of another that is strongly desired.

The Heavenly Virtue of Joy

Definition: A state of happiness or bliss. The experience of great pleasure or delight. The emotion evoked by wellbeing, success, or good fortune.

1. Being envious of almost everyone or everything they have with a total passion for possession.

    Envy is a disease of the soul. It will eat away at you like acid. You will never be content because there will always be someone who has more than you or has something you would like to have. You are bonded to the materialism of the world and completely separated from your spirit. As long as you are envious you will never have peace of mind.

2. Resentment toward some people who have what they don't have.

    If you don't have something that someone else has, it is easy to fall into a state of resentment. This, however, will eat at your soul, and you will always feel like something is missing that you should have.

3. Wishing you could have what another has or to be like them.

    It's only normal to wish for what you don't have. It's also normal to wish to be more like someone, that is to be smarter, stronger, better looking, more successful, and popular. There is nothing wrong with this as long as the wish does not become obsessive.

4.   Having no desire to be like someone or have what they have.

When you have the confidence in yourself that you have no desire to be someone other than who you are or to possess more than you already have then you are free from envy. There is a certain peace of mind that comes with a lack of envy.

5.   Finding extreme happiness in being glad for other people and what they have and for what they have accomplished.

Most people will not be able to attain number 5 since it would putting away a desire for anything material and finding your happiness in the joy of seeing other people have something. Probably the best we can aspire to is not having a desire for what others have or not needing to accomplish what they done. Again, this is moderation and will bring you a certain peace and contentment with being happy with what you have.

The Deadly Sin of Wrath and the Heavenly Virtue of Love

The Deadly Sin of Wrath

Definition: Extreme violence anger and rage

Wrath is probably one of the worse, if not the worst, sin because it combines hate, rage, and violence. The violence is usually unrestrained and leaves permanent physical and emotional scars, especially with children. Those who have wrath in their heart usually hate not only others but themselves also. They live in a state of perpetual anger which can explode at any given moment. They usually have little or no control over their anger, and violence becomes an extension of their anger.

There is always hope for anyone, however, people with wrath become a victim of their own anger before they can experience a change of heart.

The Heavenly Virtue of Love

Definition: Affection based on admiration, unselfish concern that unconditionally accepts another.

There is probably no other sin where the opposite is an extreme as in wrath and love. Some believe that God is infinite intelligence, infinite energy, and infinite love. Of these three, love is deemed to be the greatest because it holds everything together. When a person has true love in their heart, their body and soul are held together. Since number five is an almost impossible state to obtain much less to keep, then number four can be the good of choosing a clear path to spirituality.

Moderation continues to be the key. Doing the possible, number four is more than possible to both obtain and keep for the most part and should be the goal. Having true love in your heart will always result in peace of mind and a certain joy that eludes those who do not have true love in their heart.

The Degrees from Deadly Sin to Heavenly Virtue

1. Engaging in violence, living in anger and subject to fits of rage.

2. Constantly is in a state of anger or adopting and angry mood at the least little thing. Using violence as a last resort.

    There are those who always seem to be angry. They live in a state of anger. Anger controls their life. They can be angry at others, the world as it is or even themselves. They are easily provoked and will lash out over almost anything that upsets them. Violence is usually a last resort when they are venting their anger but they can and will resort to it with continued provocation.

3. Controlling your anger in most situations and always refraining from violence.

    Those who are somewhat prone to anger can control themselves the majority of time. They may be internally angry but realize that venting their anger is unacceptable behavior in most instances therefore they refrain from acting and speaking out in anger. Violence does not enter their mind as a solution to any confrontation. For the most part they may have some anger but it is concealed and kept in check.

4. Seeing others as they really are and accepting them with an absence of malice. Using kindness in place of ill feelings.

    When these people look at others and see them as they really are they make a choice. They choose to accept them as they are with an absence of any kind of malice or ill feeling. They are not judgemental of others and when they love someone they love them completely and unconditionally. They have love in their heart.

5.   Achieving a state of mind where you have love in your heart for everyone.

The highest degree of love is when you have love in your heart for everyone and maintain this love on a constant unceasing basis. No exception. This is an almost impossible stage to reach since the human factor of discretion will raise its ugly head. It is only something that we can aspire to do sometimes.

The Deadly Sin of Greed and the Heavenly Virtue of Generosity

The Deadly Sin of Greed

Definition: A ravenous desire for more than one needs or deserves as in wealth, power, or material possessions. Extreme materialism.

The Heavenly Virtue of Generosity

Definition: Liberality of giving in spirit or action.

1. Taking everything you can constantly with no consideration of others and never having enough to satisfy you.

    "Greed has its own rewards," as the old saying goes. Those who have greed in their heart can never get or have enough. They not only have the need to possess, they have the need to take from others. Therefore, they can never be satisfied. They can never have enough. They live in a perpetual state of frustration. They are slaves to their greed. This is the reward of greed. The biggest and best advantage that the confidence man has over his victim is their own greed which he plays to his ultimate advantage. In their quest for more, the greedy person falls into their own trap. If they did not have greed in their heart, they could not be taken advantage of.

2. A desire to have most of everything you want with no regard of others.

    We all have desires for things we don't or cannot have. It becomes a problem when this need or desire overrides and has no regard for others and what they have.

3.   Getting only that which you need and limiting your wants.

We all have legitimate needs wants and desires. It helps us personally if we put some sort of limit on these needs and desires. This means being satisfied with what you have and being content with less.

4.   Putting the needs and wants of others before your own.

Those who have the power to overcome the "*me*" can put others before themselves. Their own wants needs and desires can take second place to the needs and desires of others. This is the true meaning of getting past the "*me.*" This requires a state of mind where material possession have little or no importance.

5.   Total generosity to others and giving everything you have to others and possessing almost nothing you can call your own.

The opposite end of the spectrum is generosity. If we take number five to its ultimate conclusion, we would have to choose the life of a monk. Since less than five percent of people living choose this vocation, then we again must indulge in some form of moderation.

The Deadly Sin of Sloth and the Heavenly Virtue of Labor

The Deadly Sin of Sloth

Definition: Aversion to work or exertion laziness, insolence, sluggishness.

The Heavenly Virtue of Labor

Definition: Exerting one's power of body and or mind to its limit.

1.   Doing as little as is humanly possible.

    People in this category will do almost anything to avoid doing a task. They will sometimes work harder at getting out of work than the actual work itself. They are lazy about everything even the smallest personal task. This causes them to be sluggish and apathetic. Those guilty of extreme sloth have been this way their whole life and will probably be that way to the end of their life.

2.   Doing just enough to get by and exist.

    Then there are those who do only what they absolutely have to do. They will work but avoid it at all cost if possible. Their goal is simply to just do enough to just get by and absolutely no more. They make the worst and most frustrating of all employees and usually wind up getting fired. Most people don't want to work with them because they wind up doing some or all of their work.

3.   Working at a regular job with normal hours.

    These are the people who put in their eight hours, go home, and don't look for anything else to do. They are usually good and dependable workers, but don't expect them to do anything over and above their main job. They are easily content and have no great expectations.

4. Always keeping busy doing something most of the time.

    People who seem to be always busy doing something, working, reading, creating something, playing music, going out for dinner, seeing family members or friends, or just socializing, they are always occupied in some sort of endeavor. They always seem to have a purpose for their body and or mind.

5. Total dedication of body and mind in the pursuit of a worthwhile and positive goals and objectives.

    Workaholic best describes this last category. They are totally dedicated to whatever they are doing whether making money or achieving a goal. They are interesting people who make the best possible use of what God gave them all of the time. They are tireless even in old age and maintain a pace few can keep up with. They are always positive and optimistic about everything they do with an intensity that is rare. They even have trouble keeping up with themselves.

The Deadly Sin of Pride and the Heavenly Virtue of Humility

The Deadly Sin of Pride

Definition: The quality or state of being proud, inordinate self-esteem, conceit, disdainful attitude toward others, an ostentatious display of behavior, and excessive appreciation of one's worth or virtue. Obsessive.

The Heavenly Virtue of Humility

Definition: The quality or condition of being humble, lacking pride, being modest, submissive, or having self-abasement. A humble state of mind.

1. Excessive adoration of self, possessions or accomplishments, with a clear disdain for others.

   Pride is loving yourself more than anyone. Pride is believing you are better than most and equal to anyone. You can take pride in yourself or what you have accomplished. Pride is a belief you are better, what you have is better, and what you have done is better and when you put yourself above everybody, you are obsessed with the "*me.*" When you are that obsessed with yourself, you are about as far removed from a spiritual state as you can be. Pride always comes to a better end with the *fall*, and the *fall* always comes. The fall comes when you are humiliated by someone who proves beyond the shadow of a doubt he is a better person, has more, and has done more than the prideful person can even imagine. Human nature, in its eternal quest to be better, have more, and do better, will always bring forth someone who will show the prideful person up for what they are.

2.   A need to be proud of yourself and a feeling that you are better than most people.

We all need to take certain amount of pride in who we are or what we have done, but this should not lead to a feeling that we are better than other people. When we look upon ourselves as being above a lot of people, our ego will become overinflated, and we will begin to have a disdain for others. It's much harder to get past the *me* when you incur this state of mind.

3.   Taking pride in what you do or have accomplished but not yourself.

We can take pride in ourselves and what we have done without reaching the point that it's all about us. We can look at what others have done and realize that we do not have a monopoly on being better or having done more. This is the first step in the humility process.

4.   Realizing that other people have accomplished more than you and that other people have character traits that you wish you had.

When you reach the point where you can see and appreciate the character and achievement of others and see they have, in a lot of instances, far surpassed you, then you will begin to put yourself in a different and proper perspective. You can begin to get past the *me*. This alone will put you on the right road to being humble.

5.   Having a true sense of humility and being completely humble when your good points and achievements are recognized by others.

True humility can only come with the realization that we are no better than anyone. God created us all equal and imperfect. It is just a degree of imperfection that makes us different. We are better than no one. We are just different. God gave us the commandment, "Love everyone." God didn't just say love the ones you want to or the ones which you like or the ones which you feel are good people. God said everyone. When we realize we are better than no one, then and only then can we find it in our hearts to love everyone, no matter who they are or what they have done. God loves everyone regardless of their actions and characteristics. We cannot understand the depth of this love, but we can in our own imperfect way try to best imitate it. We can only achieve true humility when we consider ourselves nothing. Only then can we be truly free and have peace.

The Deadly Sin of Gluttony and the Heavenly Virtue of Fasting

Gluttony

Definition: Gross excess in eating and drinking

Fasting

Definition: Abstaining from food, eating sparingly or abstaining from some foods.

1. Unlimited overeating and drinking constantly, for pleasure.

    Gluttony can only be described as a compulsion to fill some inner need that seems to never be satisfied. It is totally selfish behavior that has become a habit and a way of life. Gluttons do not care what others think of their behavior. They only care about filling a void within that refuses to be satisfied.

2. Eating and or drinking between regular meals and at odd times when hungry.

    This would be considered overeating and having little or no control to eat whenever they are hungry. When hunger comes they will give in and eat what makes them feel good—cookies, ice cream, etc. Eating is one of the more important aspects of their life. They love and live to eat or drink.

3. Eating three healthy meals a day with drinking in moderation.

    These people eat in moderation but also eat for pleasure. They control themselves to a great degree but have a tendency to want to enjoy what they eat and gain pleasure from food. This sometimes leads to over indulgence in food they are particularly fond of. They control their eating for the most part but still eat mostly for pleasure.

4. Eating healthy meals and not eating for pure pleasure.

    When you eat for your health and do not wish to obtain pleasure from the food you eat, you are eating to live rather than living to eat. Putting away the desire to eat for pleasure requires that something in your life is more important than gaining pleasure from food. Food will have only the importance of maintaining good health and nothing more. There is nothing to gain from eating for pleasure. Pleasure is gained from other sources.

5. Fasting on a regular basis.

    Putting food aside in your life and doing completely without it is a spiritual quest. This need of the body is put aside for periods of time to get in touch with your spiritual side. This requires not only great discipline but a mind-set that can exclude food from your life for a period, one day, three days, seven days, etc., and is done on a regular basis. This is a great undertaking and is only for those who are dedicated to becoming more spiritual.

The Deadly Sin of Lust and the Heavenly Virtue of Chastity

The Deadly Sin of Lust

Definition: Excessive and unrestrained sexual craving with an obsessive desire for sexual satisfaction.

In the pursuit of spirituality, number 5 is an unreal goal even for monks who have taken the vow of chastity because your human nature will not allow you to be free of lust or sexual thoughts. You can lust in your mind and imagination, and when you do lust, no matter what form it takes, you are only considering your own wants needs and desires.

The Heavenly Virtue of Chastity

Definition: The state of being chase or pure, the practice of celibacy, and remaining a virgin.

Number four has the best chance of bringing you closer to God since you are putting yourself aside and only thinking of giving another pleasure and making another person happy other than yourself. The more you can put yourself aside the closer you will come to your spiritual side and God.

The Degrees from Deadly Sin of Lust to Heavenly Virtue of Chastity

1. Uninhibited and unrestrained sexual craving with an obsessive desire for sexual satisfaction.

    Those who exhibit his tendency use others with a total disregard of the person. They are more than capable of inflicting pain if this is what they need to satisfy themselves. They never seem to be able to achieve satisfaction and therefore continue to push the boundaries in all kinds of sexual acts. This includes having sex with children and minors.

They will engage in the lowest forms of depravity with absolutely no feeling for those the person or person they are using. Those who fall into this category are usually the worst kind of predators.

2.   Using others to fulfill your sexual desires with no thought of the other person

This person is similar to number one in the fact that they both use other people strictly for their own ends. The difference lies in the extreme to which number one goes. Both have no feeling or regard for the other person. There is no emotion, sensitivity, and caring, only raw selfish passion. This person usually does not engage in sadistic actions, only totally selfish act. They use people and toss them aside like disposable wipes. People's feeling have no meaning to them since they are devoid of feeling except for themselves.

3.   Having consensual sex with the idea in mind to achieve mutual satisfaction.

Sexual fulfillment is still the same aim except that there is a consideration for the other person in the process. It's sort of a philosophy of giving a little and taking a little. This person is thinking of the other person and realizing they can achieve what they want by extending themselves to another. This could be called unselfish-selfish behavior.

They are still using others but are willing to give something in return. Mutual satisfaction becomes more enjoyable than self-satisfaction.

4.   Having sex for the purpose of creating children in order to have a family or having sex with another person with the

sole desire to give pleasure to the other person rather than yourself.

This is putting yourself aside in the interest of your family to have children. Wanting, having, and caring for children require unselfish behavior. A family man puts his family before himself. The unselfish act of sexual love puts yourself aside and is based solely on giving someone else pleasure and making them feel good and loved. This is true love in one of its highest form. This person is able to put himself totally aside for another.

5.   Chasity and a total absence of any and all sexual pleasure.

Priests, nuns, and monks take the vow of chastity. They vow to stay chaste and abstain from any and all forms of sexual pleasure. The purpose is to bring them closer to God and to be able to concentrate entirely on the spiritual aspect of their nature. Complete and total chastity is impossible since sexual desire is man's second strongest instinct.

A person can abstain from sexual acts, maybe, but no matter how dedicated you are, sexual thoughts and impulses will come into your mind from time to time. The dedication to remain chaste is one of the highest forms of spirituality, but like humans, it is still imperfect.

The Seven Steps to a More Spiritual Life

Each of the seven steps is in tune with one of the heavenly virtues. Each step requires that you put yourself and your ego aside. It is also necessary to lessen the possessions in your life. The further you are removed from your human nature which puts you first and the obsessive need for material possession, the closer you will be to becoming a more spiritual person. You, of course, cannot put yourself aside, but you can moderate your behavior and do with less. The key to a more spiritual life is moderation as you shall see.

Step 1. The Virtue of Chastity

Complete and total chastity is a mere figment of the imagination. It is impossible simply because next to survival, it is our second strongest instinct and will not be resisted. Even if we totally refrain from sex, the desires will still invade your mind and motivate you to fulfill your impulses in one way or another. Most people on the planet engage in sexual activity, in order to have a family or enjoy the pleasure of having sex.

Sexual activity quickly becomes focused on your own pleasure to the exclusion of everything else. You put yourself and your pleasure first without even thinking. Since it is a forgone conclusion that we will be continually engaged in sexual activity, then the key to become more spiritual is to make a conscious effort to put yourself and your pleasure aside and be driven by a desire to give your partner more pleasure than you give to yourself. This is within the realm of possibility and will give you more joy that you might be able to imagine and bring you closer to your spiritual side.

Step 2. The Virtue of Fasting

This virtue has to do with eating and food. The ultimate is fasting, which can usually only be sustained for limited periods of time.

Religious people will sometimes fast for certain holy seasons such as lent. There is no doubt that fasting will bring you closer to being a more spiritual person, and it is a good thing to fast once in a while, but most people cannot or will not do this because of the way they live. When people work a regular job, have families and other responsibilities, this is just not feasible. It then comes down to food. We eat not only because it's necessary to survive, we also eat for pleasure and to satisfy other needs, such as anxiety, frustration, etc. We gain pleasure and satisfaction from food. Sometimes we eat when we are not even hungry. To become a more spiritual person, instead of living to eat, you can eat to live. This means moderating your behavior. Instead of putting yourself and the pleasure of eating first, you moderate your behavior. You can eat to live and still enjoy what you eat, but food will no longer be the most important thing in your life. You will eat what you need to eat and be satisfied. You will feel better about yourself because you will have more control over yourself. You will also feel and be physically better with this moderation in your eating habits. You will also become a more spiritual person in the process since you have put yourself and your pleasure aside and got past yourself.

Step 3. The Virtue of Humility

Wanting to feel proud of who we are and what we do comes second nature to us. The problem comes when we begin to feel better than other people and compare ourselves to other people. When that happens, we also begin to treat people in a lesser way and have less or no regard for them. We consider other people inferior and treat them as such. This fosters a high degree of self-love. We convince ourselves we are better, smarter, stronger, or faster than others, and we will do almost anything to prove it. We never can of course because there will always be some who are better, smarter, stronger, or faster.

Pride will make you put yourself over almost everything and everybody. True humility will only come when you realize that God created all people equal but different. The great commandment of love states that you love everyone. The commandment doesn't say just love the ones that you want to or the ones you like. The commandment of love is to love everyone.

You don't have to like what they do or who they are because you won't, but if you are to become more humble, then you need to feel love in your heart for everyone. The fastest but not the easiest way is to come to the conclusion that you are better than no one, different but not better. This gives your spirit the freedom to feel true love for everyone. Obviously, you will become a more spiritual person and experience a freedom of self and true joy you would have never had before. You can get past yourself and feel better about yourself.

Step 4. The Virtue of Generosity

Greed is said to be in the heart of everyone. There is always a desire to have more. Some desire to have the most, and the truly greedy person wants it all. Greed usually refers to money or things, but a person can also be greedy for power, fame, recognition, or attention. Greedy people can only be happy when they have it all, and even then happiness and contentment elude them because they always want more. In the end, happiness comes from giving, not from taking. True generosity is giving everything you have or will ever have to others. This is beyond most people since it leaves them with nothing. A person who wishes to be more spiritual will choose to give of themselves and what they have is moderation. They will always be willing to share their time, their selves, and their possessions with others.

They realize possessions only have a limited value in their life and are finite. They also realize that their time is the most precious commodity, and they are willing to share it or give it to another. When a person is able to get past the *"me"* of keeping and is willing to give, the things of this world will lose their importance. They have gotten past themselves and in losing themselves, they have gained a sense of freedom, joy, and contentment, which only their spiritual side can provide.

Step 5. The Virtue of Love

Love could be the highest of virtues since it encompasses all the other virtues. They all hinge on love of one kind or another. Those who believe in God believe in a god of love, a god who not only can but does forgive any and every one of any wrong they have committed and still love them. Our spiritual side almost demands that we have love in our heart for others. Our spiritual side also demands that we forgive others who have wronged us. We can begin to reach this spiritual side of us when we choose to have love in our hearts for others and forgive others. This is a choice we can make. When we choose to forgive another and take it one step further by saying, "It never happened," we have given ourselves freedom from resentment and grudges, both of which are like acid to the soul. True humility is accepting and believing we are better than no one. We may be different, but we are no better.

This allows us to have love in our heart for everyone and be free of judgmental and critical behavior. Giving ourselves the gift of accepting others unconditionally is one of the greatest gifts we can give ourselves besides choosing to have love in our hearts for others. Choosing to love and love unconditionally will put us in close touch with our spiritual side.

Step 6. The Virtue of Labor

Since a total of one-third of our day is spent doing work of some sort then it is only reasonable to expect that we should try to enjoy what amounts to one-third of our life. There is a sense of joy in doing something that gives us a feeling of satisfaction and of doing something well. When we can go beyond ourselves and find something of value in the work we perform and see the intrinsic good in it, then we can begin to connect with our spiritual side. When we use our minds for creating or seeing knowledge rather than engaging in selfish thoughts which tend to exclude anyone but ourselves, then we become more in tune with our spiritual nature. Our thoughts and efforts are being directed to an end which goes beyond us. Working and thinking can be more beneficial and spiritual than most people can imagine. It's all in the way we look at it and feel about it. We will always be a product of what we think. Thinking spiritual will help us to become more spiritual and happy.

Step 7. The Virtue of Joy

This virtue is a rejection of materialism as a way to find happiness. We are materialistic when all we care about is having and getting more. When and if we can reach the conclusion that the material things of this world are only temporary at best and can never bring us lasting happiness, will we be able to discount their importance? Being spiritual is being able to take or leave the things of the world. Becoming more spiritual is becoming less worldly. One hundred years from now, what we see in front of us today will not exist and neither will we. This collection of atoms and molecules will be changed in other forms or pure energy. This is a fact. We do, however, have a spirit which has eternal life. This is the best part of us. This is the part of us that will still exist after everything else in the world has gone. We are spiritual beings. We were created spiritual beings and were meant to be spiritual beings. Being more spiritual brings us into closer everlasting contact with our creator. This choice is yours to make.

The Benefits

When the benefits of doing something or having something are discussed, the cost of having or doing something is very seldom talked about. Everything has a price. If you are going to do something or have something that will benefit you, then there is a price you must pay. The cost or price must be considered before you endeavor to do something or have something which will benefit you. Should you choose to have a more spiritual life, the benefits will probably far exceed your expectations in the happiness it will bring to your life. There, however, is a cost to all this, and this cost or price needs to be considered first. You will have to pay the price of changing or modifying your life to some degree. Instead of putting yourself first and what you want first, you will have to put yourself aside most of the time. This is much easier said than done since most of us have put ourselves first all of our life. You must also put aside what you want, if not all of what you want, then some of what you want. Putting yourself aside requires discipline and a mind-set. You must set your mind to accept putting yourself and some of what you want aside. The cost of being spiritual also involves the giving of yourself to others. If you have never done this, it's not easy. Should you decide to change your life and become a more humble, loving, giving, spiritual person, then the rewards will be worth far more than the cost.

When you give of yourself freely and without expectation of receiving something in return, your heart will be filled with a joy and bliss you may have never felt before. All of the sudden, your life will have meaning where it had never had meaning before. You will feel better about yourself, about who you are and what you do. You will receive a sense of self-satisfaction that may have eluded you all of your life. You will feel true happiness for other people. You will feel more alive than ever before. Your problems will become smaller and easier to handle since you will be filled with a sense of ease and peace. Relationships with others, especially your family and those you love or care about, will take on a whole new and exciting dimension. You will appreciate those in your life with an intensity you have never felt before. You will live, laugh, and love your whole day through.

You will be more positive, optimistic, and hopeful than you have ever been, and your soul will tingle.

You will reach and touch a part of your being that is the best part of you. You will truly begin to know who you are and what you are and you will like who you are and what you are.

These are the benefits of being a spiritual person. Life is a series of never-ending choices. The choice to become a more spiritual person is yours and yours alone. You will not only benefit but everyone around you will also benefit. You will become a big ripple in the pond of life.

You will have such far-reaching effects and impact on the lives of others that it will exceed your imagination and understanding. Your ripple will never stop, ever.

References

Stager, Curt. 2014 Your Atomic Self St. Martin's Press

Alighieri, Dante. 2009 The Inferno Signet Classics

Pascal, Blaise. 1995 Penses Penguin Classics

About the Author

The author was born in Paducah Kentucky, a city on the Ohio River in the southwest corner of the state. He moved to Pittsburgh, Pennsylvania, when he was six years old. His father died when he was ten and he started to work at that age. He worked a full-time job during his high school years and enlisted in the Army on his seventeenth birthday. He was in the military police when in the service and is a veteran. When he was discharged, he worked as a laborer on construction projects and sold encyclopedias door to door. He also sold insurance, home improvements, and stocks. He started his own business, a collection agency. He also owned and started a promotional photography business and established a manufacture's representation company for the furniture industry. He has written a book titled *I Sight: Seeing Ourselves and Others as We Really Are*. This book is based on the premise that when you can know and understand yourself, then you are in a better position to know and understand other people and vice versa. The author also served as a Stephen minister and counseled people who had health and psychological problems. He is still actively employed in his own business, selling home care products. He currently lives in Georgia with his wife Max, whom he calls a saint and whom he considers to be his inspiration. He is still dealing with getting past the "*me*" in his life.

CPSIA information can be obtained
at www.ICGtesting.com
Printed in the USA
BVHW08*1307260818
525248BV00003B/15/P